PREFACE

The term *worship leader* is one that is commonly thought of as a person in leadership at a church in charge of musical worship. Although this is a true description, the worship leader can be anyone who leads others to worship God. A senior pastor is a worship leader. A church counselor is a worship leader. A Sunday school teacher is a worship leader. If we are followers of Christ, we should aim to help lead others to worship God, not just in the musical part of the church service but in all areas of life—living out lifestyle worship. Although this book focuses on the musical worship leader, the concepts in it can apply to many different areas where people lead others in lifestyle worship, as it discusses eight important roles to provide direction and encouragement with focus on the calling of being a worship leader.

LIFESTYLE WORSHIP

8 Roles of the Worship Leader

Terry Tripp

CONTENTS

For Theodore

(A Gift from God)

THE WORSHIP LEADER'S ROLE OF BEING A CHILD OF GOD

It is common for people to struggle with identity, especially naturally ambitious people who often find themselves in leadership roles. We desire knowledge. We devour information. We search for identity. Worship leaders are no exception. I, like many of my peers, personally began this struggle in high school. "Who am I?" was a question that silently lingered in the back of my mind. If I ever had the nerve to ask my parents such a complexed question, they would seek to calm my anxious mind by answering such an overwhelming question with, "That's simple; you are my son." Now, this answer was never satisfying to a teenager who was beginning to stretch his mind too far too soon. I yearned for a simple and clear identity in something. There was the built and broad, short hair Chris who was clearly the school's football jock. There was the tall, lengthy, long hair, black fingernail Ryan who played in a goth band who was the school's rock star. There was Sarah, the most popular girl in school, who you would rarely see in real life who held a celebrity status. There was the drum major, although I cannot remember his name, who was the band guy. There was Erin the track star. Like the 90's comedy *Clueless*, it felt like everyone was something, but what was I? I remember seeing shirts at a trendy clothing store that read, "Life is baseball." I thought what if I tried out and made the baseball team? Maybe I could be a baseball player. There it was, a clear-cut identity! I went to the first day of baseball conditioning with my buddy and realized quickly it was not for me when students were being pushed so hard they were falling to the ground vomiting as the coaches cussed at them in laughter.

In *Baptism: A Biblical Study*, Jack Cottrell explains the change of identity that happens when we are born again in Christ and are baptized. He states, "In the Biblical world a person's *name* was not just an arbitrary means of identification but was considered to be intrinsically related to the person himself, representing his qualities and his character and his very nature."[1] We are baptized in the name of the Father, Son, and Holy Spirit in front of our community to show we now have a new identity, and with our new identity, we represent the family name; we are Christians.

When I was in high school, I was a born-again Christian, so why did I still struggle so much with identity when I had already been baptized? The answer is simple: everything is a struggle in high school. But why do worship leaders sometimes still struggle with identity today? Let us discuss our fictional worship leader. We can call him Thomas; that is a nice biblical name. Thomas has been married for seven years, has two young children and a beautiful wife who sometimes sings with the worship team from time to time but does not always get along with the other women on the team. He just found out that his younger daughter is autistic. He is employed fulltime at the church as the church's contemporary worship leader where the younger half of the church sees him as their hero/advocate of modern music while the other half of the church sees him as a wolf in sheep's clothing who is secretly planning on erasing their beloved hymns from church history. He is in his early thirties and is already losing too much hair to feel confident being streamed online with HD, full-face closeups. He and his wife just purchased their first house, which is a fixer upper. He quickly changes his outfit from skinny jeans and a V-neck shirt when he leads worship for the early morning high school group to more lose jeans and a collar neck shirt for the 11:00 blended/contemporary service after the senior pastor had spoken to him about several complaints about his irreverent dress attire. His week is full of busy tasks including preparing the snow cone maker for the church's carnival to making sure the Bible verses on the projection screen match the same version that the senior pastor is using that week. With family obligations at home and a packed schedule at work, he tries to pray through the stress of financial worries and tosses around the idea of going to seminary to get a MDiv, so he might be able to apply to be a pastor someday. On his tired drive home from work, he reminisces about his younger days of less responsibilities and takes a prayerful detour. He silently asks, "Who am I?" He remembers the Scripture he has hidden in his heart, the words of the Apostle Paul from Galatians 3:26-29 (ESV): "[F]or in Christ Jesus you are all sons of God, through faith. For as many of you as were baptized into Christ have put on Christ. There is neither Jew nor Greek, there is neither slave nor free, there is no male and female, for you are all one in Christ Jesus. And if you are Christ's, then you are Abraham's offspring, heirs according to promise." Thomas mouths quietly along in his car, "I am a child of God," and he drives home to love and serve his family, remembering how blessed he really is.

   I teach at a school on the other side of town about half an hour away. There and back, I drive about an hour a day. If you add up that time, it is roughly five hours a week. That is a lot of time, so I dedicated part of my morning drive to prayer. I began this with my regular prayer checklist that I routinely offered everything up that I was worried about. I then felt the Holy Spirit tell me to start ending my prayers by praying that God helps me know and live as a true child of his. Above all else, I am a child of God. Before we are husbands, fathers, employees, worship leaders, we are children of God. This is our first role in life, to be God's child and to know that he is our Father. If we forget this or put it lower on our identity list, we are not authentic worship leaders to others.

In *Worship: The Ultimate Priority*, John MacArthur states, "... the sad truth is that such a distorted concept of worship is actually easier to find nowadays than authentic worship based on sound, biblical principles."[2] Worship leaders must make being a child of God a priority by studying and meditating on sound, biblical doctrine, having an active and personal prayer life, and by having encouraging relationships with other believers. These spiritual disciplines work together to mold people into being leaders of real worship as they fully understand and share their role of being a child of God. MacArthur explains, "Real worship therefore should be the full-time, nonstop activity of every believer, and the aim of the exercise ought to be to please *God*, not merely entertain the worshiper."[3] Unfortunately, there are people who lead worship today who do not have a solid foundation in the Word of God, do not spend time in prayer, and only participate in superficial fellowship at best. They sing that they are a child of God, but their hearts seek identities that are common to secular thought.

In *The Church in an Age of Crisis: 25 New Realities Facing Christianity*, James Emery White states, "When it comes to Christianity, people just don't know much."[4] There was once a time in our American culture where the common layperson could recite the Ten Commandments, name all the disciples, tell the story of Moses, and explain the essence of the gospel of Christ. Today, people might be able to recite John 3:16 and questionably state, "Doesn't the Bible say something about loving everyone?" Although Christians are not the common laypeople, they have suffered from the contemporary generation's lack of Bible knowledge. For example, I can recall casually talking to my grandma in Oklahoma on the phone, asking her what she was doing. She explained how she was going through the Bible with her notepad and writing out the generational chronology of all the main characters in Scripture. Doing such an activity in her spare time, one might think she were a scholar or academic instructor, but she was never even a university student. She was raised during a time when the culture placed a strong importance on the value of Scripture.

When modern-day Christians place value on the import-ance of Bible study, there is sometimes an imbalance of prayer. I am sure most people who have spent years in the church have come across the Christian who just loves to debate doctrine but lacks the heartfelt desire to encourage and serve people through being a beacon of light that comes with a dedicated prayer life. I have heard people ask, "Why do I need to pray when God is omnis-cient?" Although books have been dedicated to this question, the simple answer is this: because Christ told us to. He prayed, and we are to be like him.

One of the most powerful set of verses in the New Testa-ment is when we see how Jesus prayed when he prayed for us in John 17:20-23:

> I do not ask for these only, but also for those who will be-lieve in me through their word, that they may all be one, just as you, Father, are in me, and I in you, that they also may be in us, so that the world may believe that you have sent me. The glory that you have given me I have given to them, that they may be one even as we are one, I in them and you in me, that they may become perfectly one, so that the world may know that you sent me and loved them even as you loved me.

Christ desires for us to be as one, but the world teaches us we can do it on our own. You can recognize the influence of the enemy by seeing his footprint of division. The enemy loves to divide and isolate believers, so they are vulnerable to an attack. I shared a video during a Bible study once that showed a lion at-tacking a gazelle. The lion did not attack the gazelle in a large group but patiently waited for it to be distant from the pack. As soon as enough division took place and there was an ample amount of distance between the lone gazelle and its pack, the vi-cious lion attacked its prey. Worship leaders must never be the lone gazelle, or they will be seriously attacked, and sadly, many are. To continue to grow spiritually, worship leaders should have their inner circle of friends. Of course they are going to have a large community of friendly acquaintances, but their inner circle is the God-given few who they can depend on through personal struggles and life's tragedies. This group not only sees your dirty laundry, but they help wash it.

When I was a high school student, I clearly remember my youth pastor putting up a twenty-foot banner that displayed the text, "Don't go it alone," with abstract paint splatters all around the font. Although he only taught about it on occasion, the large words behind the worship band made an impact in my mind to work earnestly to hold onto friendships, even when they let you down from time to time. Many times in my life the enemy would whisper in my ear, "Look how they let you down; you don't need them." Then I would be reminded by those words, "Don't go it alone." Do not be the lone gazelle. Be the answer to Jesus' prayer by being one with our brothers and sisters in Christ.

When worship leaders focus on spiritual discipline, they are investing into their own personal relationship with the Father, which must always come first. God is worthy of our first, and until we understand our first role of being a worship leader is being a child of God, we will not be able to authentically lead others, no matter how many times we sing it.

THE WORSHIP LEADER'S ROLE OF BEING A SPIRITUAL LEADER

When the apostle Paul gives Timothy the qualifications for being an overseer in the church, he includes the following in 1 Timothy 3:4-5: "He must manage his own household well, with all dignity keeping his children submissive, for if someone does not know how to manage his own household, how will he care for God's church?" It is clear from these verses that overseers must be able to manage their own families first to be capable of caring for the church, but I believe there is another point that can be taken from this section. If leaders are not able to manage their own family, their focus and care should be spent on their own family before the church. In Spiritual Leadership: Principles of Excellence for Every Believer, J. Oswald Sanders states, "While a leader cares for church and mission, he must not neglect the family, which is his primary and personal responsibility."[5] There is an order of priority that is given to Christians in the Bible: God, spouse, children, family, then others. And no, this is not selfish. In the same biblical book, Paul also states, "But if anyone does not provide for his relatives, and especially for members of his household, he has denied the faith and is worse than an unbeliever" (1 Timothy 5:8). From Scripture it is clear that God has priorities for his followers, especially his leaders.

If you want to tell a true godly man from a great performer, spend some time with his family. In *Worship Leaders, We are Not Rock Stars*, Stephen Miller explains: "It all belongs to Him. It's all by Him, through Him, and to Him. And who He is demands our worship in every arena of our lives."[6] Every part of a worship leader's life should aim to reflect lifestyle worship, especially the homelife. Obviously, worship leaders are male and female, but being a male, I am going to speak mostly about male worship leaders because that is what I am familiar with. When I began teaching high school art, I conducted a private study. Every time I had a male student who would be constantly rebellious and display deep feelings of anger, I looked up his family history on the school's attendance software. Just about every time I noticed there was no father listed in the student's family information. The same did not seem true for my high school female students, but I did notice that it did hold true for my female students who constantly broke school dress code. Obviously, this was not a valid study, and I had some outstanding students who also were missing fathers in their homes, but from my life experience, I have had twenty-year-old and even thirty-year-old male friends who have spoken to me with tear-filled eyes due to an absent or abusive father.

Attacking the family unit and destroying the spiritual head of the household has been the enemy's goal since the beginning. Adam and Eve went against their Father's commandment to believe a serpent instead. Then with a sin-filled world, sinful fathers failed to reflect the love of our perfect Heavenly Father. But the church should be different—*should*. Followers of Jesus should hold highly to the responsibility of being fathers to their children, so their children can easily understand the comparison of their earthly father to their heavenly Father. Let us pray for all those who cringe when they hear the word *father* and do not fully understand what it is like to have a *daddy*—an *abba*. If you want to change your life, have a child. If you want to change the world, be a daddy.

When I studied psychology as an undergraduate student, I studied a concept called *invisible work*. Invisible work is the work that people do that is hardly ever seen or recognized. Like pastors, worship leaders are often on stage in the spotlight, so although they are prime suspects of criticism, they also receive a lot of praise for work well done. If worship leaders lose a few pounds or get a new haircut, these are often commented on by the people in the service. At home the bulk of the invisible work begins. From changing the diapers of a newborn to putting out the dog late at night, there are many tasks and forms of work that go without praise. Worship leaders need to be at peace without receiving recognition for work. Yes, writing a new powerful song may bring hundreds to tears during the worship service and could even land the worship leader a record deal, but he needs to be content when he has to sacrifice such goals for the invisible work of being the spiritual leader of his family. The truth about invisible work is that although it may be invisible to others, it is not invisible to the Lord. It will be visible in the future spiritual health of the family. In time it always becomes clear which worship leader truly worked hard to lead his family in worship on stage and off stage.

One major mistake many well-intended worship leaders make is being a father first and a husband second. This completely negates the team that the husband and wife are designed to be. Do not think you are being the father of the year for putting your child first. One of the best parenting practices you can have is letting your children grow up in a home where it is completely clear that their father loves their mother dearly and puts her first. This is evident in Ephesians 5:25-27: "Husbands, love your wives, as Christ loved the church and gave himself up for her, that he might sanctify her, having cleansed her by the washing of water with the word, so that he might present the church to himself in splendor, without spot or wrinkle or any such thing, that she might be holy and without blemish." It is interesting that after Paul states this, he then says in verse 31, "Therefore a man shall leave his father and mother and hold fast to his wife, and the two shall become one flesh." From this part of Scripture, one can see that when a husband loves his wife properly, his children will observe and learn from the good example, and therefore, grow up to leave home and do the same.

Your main partner in ministry is your wife, not your senior pastor, not your guitarist or drummer. If you do not feel that your wife is a partner in ministry, then that is a sign that your marriage may need some attention. It is okay to be different in style, preferences, and even certain opinions, but husband and wife should be on the same page when it comes to ministry. Sanders states, "To reach this goal, a spouse must fully share the leader's spiritual aspirations and be willing to join in the necessary sacrifices."[7] Like with any goal in life, sacrifices will come in ministry.

I will always remember Galen Norsworthy, my Bible study teacher from church during my college years, say, "In life you'll suffer for doing good, or you'll suffer for doing bad, but when you suffer for doing good, there's a joy that is in it" (paraphrased). When worship leaders sacrifice for their wives and families, there is a joy that comes with it. For example, when people get married, others condescendingly make statements like, "No more going out with the guys to have fun. From now on you'll have to hang out with your wife." No, I *get* to spend time with my wife. Far too often foolish statements in jest are made against marriage and family that really are lies straight from the enemy. One of my friends in his thirties, a family guy with several children, explained to me sadly that his wife has Multiple Sclerosis. He expressed how he cherishes every moment with her and stares at her as she sleeps in bed next to him not being able to imagine life without her. He is not sad about spending time with her over the guys on a Friday night.

When my wife and I had our son, she was at risk of preterm labor. Everyday our son stayed in was a small victory that we checked off week after week. With my wife on bedrest for ten weeks, our son came only a week early. I had always heard of the difficulties of having a child, the never-ending diaper changes and the constant crying. After the delivery the hospital moved us to a recovery room upstairs. For that first day, he was not crying or needing a diaper change. He was very lethargic. My wife and I were worried and praying for him to cry and have a bowel movement. Eventually, he did, and I told myself that I would never complain about my son crying or needing a diaper change. Having a family is a blessing that we are not guaranteed and a blessing that not everyone gets to experience. Be thankful always, for time is always too short.

Have your family be a part of the larger church family. In *Can't Wait for Sunday: Leading Your Congregation in Authentic Worship*, Michael Walters states, "The family that eats together really does stay together."[8] He then discusses the Eucharist with explaining, "And when we share our family meal—the Eucharist —we who barely knew one another become bonded as friends, brothers, and sisters." Children who grow up in a church have the advantages of having an extended church family that many others do not have. They receive positive attention and mentorship from a great variety of people with different stories. When my sister and I grew up in church, one of our church family members was an older black woman named Velma. We called her Aunt Velma because she felt like a real aunt to us. I remember her standing next to me at my grandma's funeral and singing a closing song at the end of the funeral. She told me that although she could never replace my grandmother that I was welcome to call her anytime to talk as I did with my grandmother. I really appreciated such a kind offer. When I was a teenager, my sister, being seven years younger than me, really believed that she was our aunt, and my mom had to eventually explain to her that she was just like an aunt but was not her biological aunt. If it really takes a village to raise a child, the church is the ideal place for children to grow up as they can have those relationships that help grow a child in the ways of spiritual maturity, especially if they have smaller biological families.

Being a worship leader who is also a strong spiritual leader of your family is not an easy task. The enemy is going to do his best to take down the spiritual leader of the household. Men already often have a difficult time opening up about their struggles, and many men feel weary about having close, intimate friendships with other men. One of my best friends and I used to go out and grab dinner all the time when we were in college, but now if we are out to dinner together, some people awkwardly assume a relationship that is more than a friendship. Hence, many adult males do not have close relationships with other men, and they are socially isolated when it comes to brotherly relationships where they can discuss their personal complexities. Yes, men have their wives, which are their true best friend and partner in ministry, but sometimes men need to have uplifting brotherly fellowship, just like women need their social time with female friends. If you look at a typical Christian home though, it is common to see the wife talking on the phone to her female friends while the guy sits alone. Male worship leaders need guy friends, but like with most relationships, this will take careful choosing, time, and investment. These safe relationships are important for the health of the spiritual leader for outside accountability and encouragement because having a family is a great blessing, but it is also hard.

If you have been in church long enough, you have likely seen someone in the church give up the fight for their family and abandon their commitment and calling. One of the largest disappointments I have experienced with another person was when one of my good friends kicked out his wife because he was not feeling sexually fulfilled. I was his best man in his wedding. People do not understand how many people they negatively affect and harm when they break such a commitment. It is not just their own business.

If a job is too hard or too stressful where it is damaging your marriage, quit. If finances are weighing your marriage down, sell the car and house. If your environment is hurting your marriage, move. If an outside relationship is threatening your marriage, set up boundaries that reach the sky. Second from your relationship with God is your marriage. Treat it as such. Talk with your wife, and get to know her all over again because just like you, she is changing as well. Understand that you nor her are perfect and that although you are a worship leader who most likely married very well, neither of you are without sin, so neither of you should be without grace. Any marriage that is based on the idea that both husband and wife need to put in their part is already doomed. There is no part; each is to put in their all. In Ephesians 5:28, Paul states, "In the same way husbands should love their wives as their own bodies. He who loves his wife loves himself." If you do not continue to choose to love your wife, you are not serving her or yourself in anyway, and your children, along with the body of Christ will suffer, even if you do not see the consequences until years down the road. From many years of working as a high school teacher, I have seen the outcome of divorce in the grieving faces of teenagers already facing a trying time in their adolescence. They may force a smile at home to try to comfort a stressed parent, but I have too often seen the pain they wear when they think no one cares enough to see them.

The sad truth about children is that they are eventually going to leave you, which is exactly what they are supposed to do. So do your best with them every moment while you have them with you, but remember someday, it is just going to be you and your wife. So keep them second. I remember my dad and mom telling me that they were going to go out to dinner and watch a movie on a date when I was in high school. I was not invited. I was a little surprised at first, but as I stayed home that night watching my little sister, I was actually really happy for them. My dad taking my mom out on dates really set an example of how Christian men are supposed to continue to pursue their wives, even years into marriage. My parents loved each other and loved us. They brought us up in the way of the Lord but did not force us to believe anything. They stirred up careful conversations and replied in patience. I always think of Proverbs 22:6 when I think of their parenting practices: "Train up a child in the way he should go; even when he is old he will not depart from it." Now this is a proverb, so it is not a guaranteed promise, but most of the time it is true. Raise your children in the harshness and grace of truth. Have an understanding and patient heart, an encouraging tongue, and lifestyle that shows your trust in the Lord as you live out what it means to worship God in all things. Your example will be stronger than you can possibly imagine. Continue to do this without ceasing, and when the pain seems too great to bear, have your praise be even greater.

After graduating from high school, I visited a home Bible study that a couple held at their house on Sunday evenings. The husband would take the guys into the living room, and the wife would teach the girls in the formal living room. I remember the husband asking, "If you could have any one word written on your tombstone, what would you want it to be?" Of course, the room of college-age guys made some jokes and a few answered seriously with words like "successful" and "brilliant." It was not long until they eagerly wanted to hear his answer, and he said, "If I could have any word written on my tombstone to represent my entire life, I would be so happy to have that word be *faithful*." In being a worship leader fulfilling the role of the spiritual leader of your family, aim to be faithful—not perfect, not successful, not recognized, but faithful.

THE WORSHIP LEADER'S ADMINIS-TRATIVE ROLE

Worship leaders have an important administrative role in the church, but they are not the senior pastor. They should remember that they are there to serve the senior pastor as what Dave Williams refers to as a "number two" in How to Help Your Pastor Succeed: Moving from the Multitude to the Inner Circle.[9] He states, "When Christians learn how to be 'number two,' a church can move forward much faster than if people drag their feet and feel resentment."[10] The bright spotlight and center stage that comes with being a musical worship leader playing songs in a new style that energetically moves people in excitement can cause temptation for worship leaders to misguidedly feel that in some tiny way it is about them, but it is not. Worship leaders need to embrace the servant-hearted mindset that they are always number two, not meaning a literally second but meaning not first. Worship leaders obviously serve God first, and in the church setting, they are not only under God but under the senior pastor too. There should never be any rebellious idea of overthrowing the senior pastor or taking over the church to make it operate the way you prefer. If the church is that far off, leave it and find or start a better one.

As a musical worship leader in the church, there are going to be people who fall under your authority. There are going to be people who depend upon your leadership skills to teach, encourage, protect, and guide. You will likely be a role model to some if not many. I can recall going to Taco Bell after church one Sunday with my worship team, and two parents came up to us and asked if we would say hi to their children because their children really wanted to meet us but were too shy. So be on guard, as a worship leader, you are being watched when you do not know it.

Most people serving in ministry are doing so voluntarily. They have fulltime jobs, careers, and families with heavy responsibilities, but still they are giving their time and energy, so worship leaders must be very cognizant of their time. Musical practices need to be prompt and organized. If some want to hang around after practice and jam out for fun or fellowship, have it be optional. Remember that although your ministry might be one of the most important parts of your life, others might not feel the same, and that is okay. Successful worship leaders have the social and leadership skills to be able to encourage their musical team to practice and prepare without feeling like it is a mandate but an honor, for it is truly special to be a part of helping lead others in musical worship. A challenge for worship leaders is to teach a counter-cultural idea of playing music. Where rock star musicians on a stage in the secular world would openly receive praise, the musical team in a church does the exact opposite; they work to guide all praise and adulation to God.

Probably one of the most difficult parts of being a worship leader is knowing when and how to confront conflict. Most dedicated worship leaders I have known have had to sit down with a team member to discuss issues with sin and even give that team member some time off for counsel and healing to be fully ready to lead again. Just like God's goal for our lives, we should aim for restoration in troubling times when worship team members fall into sin. It is not about punishment. The worship leader is not looking to say, "I caught you!" but is looking to say, "How can I help you?" But to be able to successfully do this, having good relationships with your team members is key. In *How Successful People Lead: Taking Your Influence to the Next Level*, John Maxwell states, "Relationships are a major key to success, whether you're trying to sell, coach, teach, lead, or simply navigate the daily tasks of life."[11] I remember speaking to a friend who played on a worship team with me many years ago who fell into sexual sin. He explained to me how his pastor called him out privately. I asked him what the pastor said. My friend replied that the pastor told him the church was going to get him the help and accountability he needed to restore him and in time get him back leading worship once he was mentally and spiritually healthy enough to lead others. It was about three months later that I saw my friend back up on the stage playing the acoustic guitar, and I was so proud of the church for being a church that was restorative instead of damning.

There are countless other responsibilities that worship leaders have in their administrative roles. Songs should be prepared to coincide with the pastor's message. This is not just choosing the most popular and catchy tunes but analytically evaluating all of each song's lyrics to make sure they are suitable for the particular message that week and that they line up to the doctrine's the church believes and teaches. This is a high responsibility because although some people will be intensely listening to the pastor's sermon during that hour time period, they might be singing the lyrics of the worship songs all week long or even their entire lives. In *Worship Leaders, We are Not Rock Stars*, Stephen Miller explains the importance of learning to sing even the simplest songs such as "Jesus Loves Me," "Jesus Loves the Little Children," "This Little Light of Mine." He expresses, "Those simple songs were the bedrock for my childlike faith. If no one else loved me, I knew Jesus did."[12] Song choice is not simple. It must be carried out in biblical preparation with the pastor's message and guided by the Holy Spirit.

Along with song choice and preparation, come many other administrative tasks. These can include purchasing, downloading, and printing music, learning and utilizing software and mobile apps that organize musical practices, working with the sound team to properly set up the stage and balance the mix, personally learning and practicing music, and many others. Overall, the administrative role of a worship leader is almost never done, and even if it is, it all starts over again after Sunday. Therefore, worship leaders must work to find joy in these many daily tasks, which can come with the true calling for the position of the worship leader.

Colossians 3:23 states, "Whatever you do, work heartily, as for the Lord and not for men." Although this is true for everything we do, we especially need to work heartily in our administrative duties when we are directly employed by a church. The people who we are serving are also the ones who God has called to pay salaries. Nonetheless, the average church member does not have authority over you in comparison to your overseeing pastors, although some may think they do. This is similar to the unfortunate sight of a police officer pulling over someone for speeding and then the person yelling at the police officer that he pays his salary through taxes or the parent who makes strong demands from her child's teacher and reminds her that she pays her salary through taxes. The truth behind this thinking is that like the police officer and schoolteacher, worship leaders work to serve others, but that does not mean they are under everyone's authority. More than being under the authority of official overseeing pastors of the church, worship leaders are under the authority of God. They must be true and obedient to God prior to any common member, and therefore, worship leaders will make people upset and angry. It is inevitable.

New reasons for why church-goers get angry develop under new disguises, but they always come down to either miscommunication or to people not truly worshiping God but themselves instead. With people from all different backgrounds, cultures, and ages, the church can be the perfect place where miscommunication takes place, but Christians must be taught to communicate. Acts 2:1-4 states,

When the day of Pentecost arrived, they were all together

in one place. And suddenly there came from heaven a sound like a mighty rushing wind, and it filled the entire house where they were sitting. And divided tongues as of fire appeared to them and rested on each one of them. And they were all filled with the Holy Spirit and began to speak in other tongues as the Spirit gave them utterance.

When the Holy Spirit filled the early church, people from different backgrounds, cultures, and ages were able to communicate the gospel message. The church today still has the Holy Spirit, but people in it sometimes do not communicate well. They are quick tempered, impatient, and easy to get offended; they lack a servant-centered heart of grace. Some in the church need to go back to their roots, and worship leaders and church pastors can help lead the way through a practice of authentic prayer and the teaching of the Word.

As people prayerfully study God's word, the response is worship. In *Called to Worship: The Biblical Foundations of Our Response to God's Call*, Vernon Whaley states, "Our instinctive response in knowing God personally is *worship*. And worship is His strategic plan for all creation."[13] This can be illustrated in taking in a deep breath of air. It is only a matter of time until that air must be exhaled. When we inhale the Word of God, worship is what comes out. If people in the congregation are getting upset over the worship leader not choosing their preferred song selection or not choosing their child to sing on a special Sunday, they are really worshiping themselves by putting their own desires first. People who are authentically worshiping God may not always be the ones on the stage, but they definitely are not going to be the ones complaining and causing problems within the church. One of the main goals of the church should be to teach, help, and encourage people to worship God with every part of their lives. Some in the congregation will grow and learn this, but others will not and continue to be upset and complain, and you will likely be one of the many they will complain about. During such conflicts and frustrations, remember to be heavenly minded on the overall goal of leading people in worship while you seek encouragement from deep friendships with people you can be vulnerable with and trust.

THE WORSHIP LEADER'S COUNSELING ROLE

Part of being a leader of worship is having the heart of a counselor. This is being a minister of reconciliation, living with the calling of restoring the world, people, and their relationships through Christ. Mending broken relationships and coaching people through life are mental and spiritual needs of all people although many will never seek out this kind of counseling and life coaching. Although worship leaders are not typically licensed marriage-family therapists or psychiatrists, they can guide people through walking through the basics of Scripture, so people's decisions and paths are pure and line up to the will of God and the personal calling of their individual lives. There may be times in people's lives where they should seek licensed help, especially if medication is needed. Worship leaders should help their congregation dissolve the negative stigma that those who need counseling are mentally unstable and unreliable. In Overcoming the Dark Side of Leadership: How to Become an Effective Leader by Confronting Potential Failures, Gary McIntosh and Samuel Rima state,

> If you have taken the time and effort required to adequately plumb the depths of your past and have identified any child-

hood or adolescent experiences that may be dictating your behavior today; and if you have accepted the reality that you do indeed possess a dark side, no matter where on the continuum from mild to acute it falls; if you have taken the steps to address your past the best that you are able; yet you still find no relief from or control over your dark side, it is probably an indication that you need some objective outside help.[14]

Everyone has dark sides/parts of their lives that are hidden and difficult. Sometimes these stay forgotten and forgiven in the past, but often they resurface in different ways. McIntosh and Rima add, "Leaders tend to think, however, that they do not need such help and that they can work through their struggles on their own. Pastors have no problem referring parishioners to counseling, often lauding the benefits that can be gained, yet they are often hesitant to access this very helpful source themselves."[15]

Leaders and pastors can benefit greatly from the counsel of other mature believers and from biblical counseling. Worship leaders should not neglect offering counsel to their pastors and other leaders on their church staff. At the very least, worship leaders can provide words of encouragement with an offer to listen. A closed mouth and an open ear go a long way in helping people through times of frustration and pain.

Let us be clear of what biblical counseling is not. Biblical counseling is not telling others how to run their lives. It is not even necessarily giving them the answers that they seek, but it is guiding them to come to the truth through Scripture. Counselors are not directions on the map, but they are teachers to show how to read the map. If you have been called by God to be a leader of worship, then you are also called to deliver his holy Word, which brings reconciliation and healing. In *The Quick-Reference Guide to Biblical Counseling*, Tim Clinton and Ron Hawkins explain, "He has chosen you as a vessel for delivery of His special grace; you have both the privilege and responsibility to deliver that care in the most excellent and ethical way possible."[16] In Matthew 11:28-30, Christ gives the invitation: "Come to me, all who labor and are heavy laden, and I will give you rest. Take my yoke upon you, and learn from me, for I am gentle and lowly in heart, and you will find rest for your souls. For my yoke is easy, and my burden is light." Through counseling, worship leaders can help people experience the rest that is found only in Jesus in an anxious world that seldom slows down.

Being available is key. Live with an attitude where you let others know that you are available if they need you. Some people always appear to be running out the door. They never make eye contact. They take pride in their busy lifestyle as if they are scoring more points with God by juggling more and heavier objects. Busy or not, if you portray this attitude to people, they will not seek your counsel, but there are ways to change this portrayal. When you greet people, do not be the first one to look away. Add a follow up question after they tell you that they are *good*. Linger with people to allow opportunity for them to share their lives and to seek your counsel.

One of my good friends is a firefighter named Ross. He is a solid brother in Christ, but he is a quiet brother in Christ. We both create and enjoy visual art, so I began inviting him to ride with me when I would drop off a painting in Los Angeles for an art exhibition. He has joined me on several deliveries, and we have even participated in group art shows together. I knew Ross before the long drives, but I really got to know him during the heavy-traffic, Los Angeles adventures we spent in the car. He opened up to me to provide him counsel, and he provided me counsel as well. It was truly a Proverbs 27:17 experience: "Iron sharpens iron, and one man sharpens another."

There is no arrogance in biblical counseling. The counselor is not better than the person being counseled. The counselor is not all-knowing or perfect. A biblical counselor is simply a spirit-led worshiper of Jesus who has experienced suffering and pain too and still does. Clinton and Hawkins explain about spirit-led counseling, "This also reveals a compassionate empathy that can deeply relate to other because you too have walked a path of suffering and pain and yet have not turned bitter or cynical."[17]

A goal that every believer should aim for is to not become bitter with age and experience. The longer we live, the more time we have to experience happy and sorrowful moments. We will all have to make the choice to naturally allow ourselves to become callused or to joyfully look forward to the hope that we have in Jesus Christ. Paul reaffirms this in 2 Corinthians 4:16-18:

> So we do not lose heart. Though our outer self is wasting away, our inner self is being renewed day by day. For this light momentary affliction is preparing for us an eternal weight of glory beyond all comparison, as we look not to the things that are seen but to the things that are unseen. For the things that are seen are transient, but the things that are unseen are eternal.

In secular counseling the goal is typically about this current life, but in biblical counseling worship leaders help people understand that present goals in this life are good, but our real hope is beyond this temporary life. As the secular world clings on tightly to hopeful possibilities of anything eternal, followers of Christ know the only way to eternal and abundant life.

When people visit a cemetery, different sections can be seen. There are the newer graves that often display flowers or a stuffed animal. In December there might be little Christmas decorations laying on a name or a heart-shaped decoration near Valentine's Day. On the older graves, the ones that are over a hundred years old, there is typically nothing. Those people's children's children have even passed away. Eventually with a large enough expanse of time, every common person is forgotten. How about the famous person, the Hollywood celebrity, the brilliant inventor, or the record-breaking super-star? Their names might be remembered, and there might be some recorded video of them and some information about their basic characteristics written about in a biography, but their true essence is forgotten. C. S. Lewis shared so much about himself through his stories and his writings on God, but does anyone today know C. S. Lewis like his good friends or his mother and father did? Does anyone know what it was like to have him walk into the room and smile? Does anyone know what it was like to spend an hour with him in conversation over tea? At best, people will learn things about you after you are gone, but they will not truly know you. No matter what, this life is temporary. Our only hope for eternal life is in our savior. Worship leaders counsel people through Scripture to understand his enteral grace.

With the many demands of being a worship leader, one cannot neglect the counseling that takes place in the family. Some worship leaders and pastors are eager to help reconcile conflict in others' families but act as if their own extended family members are beyond help. A worship leader must never believe anyone is beyond help. Yes, it may appear that way when all the facts are examined, but God is bigger than the facts. He can do big things. He does big things.

Within the immediate family, the worship leader should make restoration of relationships a priority, even in the finest detail. Family relationships often do not fade all at once but by minor hurt feelings snowballing into a grand dilemma. Although biblical authority exists in the family structure, it still must be handed with humility and grace with the eager desire to mend together instead of tear apart. In most cases we can see the work of the enemy by division, and we can see the work of the Holy Spirit by unity. If the family is breaking apart, somewhere the enemy has had his way. If marriage breaks apart, the enemy has won a victory. Paul says in Ephesians 4:26-27: "Be angry and do not sin; do not let the sun go down on your anger, and give no opportunity to the devil." Be the one in your family that says, "Hold on, let's talk about this." Be the one who knows how to listen to others and the Holy Spirit at the same time. Be gentle in your strong stance on truth. Be a peacekeeper when you can—a minister of reconciliation as you lead. But do not wear yourself out counseling as a worship leader at work to come home and neglect your own family. I can still hear my grandmother quote to me 1 Timothy 5:8 as she prepared me as a young boy to be a future spiritual leader of a family: "But if anyone does not provide for his relatives, and especially for members of his household, he has denied the faith and is worse than an unbeliever."

One of the more obvious places where the worship leader should be a counselor is with the worship team. Consisting of dedicated Christian musicians with a single purpose in mind to create music to help the church musically worship the Lord, such a team of unique individuals playing different instruments from different backgrounds will eventually have some creative and/or personality differences. Hopefully, everyone on the team has the same goal in mind of glorifying God, but it may look different to different people, or they might want to take different paths to the same destination. To reconcile disagreements the worship leader can help bridge the communication gap that often exists in disagreements, bringing focus to the overall goal of the team and the spirit-led direction of the specific church. There are acceptable different styles of worship, but there is also false worship and wrong worship that John MacArthur explains in *Worship: The Ultimate Priority*: "A second kind of unacceptable worship is *the worship of the true God in a wrong form.* [18] When false and wrong worship is encouraged from a member on the worship team, the worship leader must step in immediately in correction. But when there is disagreement over style and method of worshiping God in spirit and truth, the worship leader then counsels, so any hurt relationships on the team can be restored through clear communication. Through the sounds of many different instruments, the team needs to be playing for the same purpose on the same path with the same goals.

Many years ago when I played lead guitar on my church's worship team, there was a season when my worship leader and I would meet up for lunch once a week. During this time we discussed the direction of the team, specific songs, their meanings, and random frustrations in life. We did not meet for *counseling*, but there was counsel that was being offered in both directions. To this day I am not sure what I appreciated more about the encouraging meetings: his advice and biblical views on life or the fact that he valued me enough to take time out of this busy schedule to spend with me.

Worship leaders having the heart of a counselor is not just for the Christian church. The secular workplace needs Christians who are leaders of worship to counsel people who are hurting and lost. Many today live under the *mind your own business* philosophy of life, but with high depression and suicide rates, this life philosophy is not working. Although most will never ask for counsel, direction, or any type of guidance, they are in dire need of it. It is easy to offer a homeless man twenty dollars, but what if people sat down with him to get to know him to offer him encouragement through wise counsel? We probably cannot expect the common person to do this, but if anyone is going to sit down with a stranger to hear about his life and offer him encouragement and direction, should it not be the same person who is called to live a life of directing people to worship God? The world needs counsel too, and some listen with open hears and open hearts. Others will reject it, and they will reject you. But people rejected Jesus too.

THE WORSHIP LEADER'S TEACHING AND DISCIPLING ROLE

There is a misunderstanding about the great commission in some evangelical churches. They teach that the great commission is to tell as many people as possible about Jesus. This may seem good at first glance, but it is lacking in full biblical content. In Matthew 28:18-20, Jesus says, "All authority in heaven and on earth has been given to me. Go therefore and make disciples of all nations, baptizing them in the name of the Father and of the Son and of the Holy Spirit, teaching them to observe all that I have commanded you. And behold, I am with you always, to the end of the age." Making disciples requires a lot of work but is sometimes replaced with handing out a paper track pamphlet or a flyer invitation to church instead. The disciples that Jesus made required a lot of investment—a lot of teaching. Being called to be like Christ, worship leaders are not exempt from the great commission of teaching and discipling.

When Jesus' parents lost him in Jerusalem after the Feast of the Passover when he was only twelve, Luke 2:46-47 states, "After three days they found him in the temple, sitting among the teachers, listening to them and asking them questions. And all who heard him were amazed at his understanding and his answers." Jesus was teaching them by listening, asking questions, and giving answers. His example provides a helpful method of teaching and discipling. We first listen, then ask questions to inspire thought, and then provide answers—truth.

In *The 5 Levels of Leadership: Proven Steps to Maximize Your Potential*, John Maxwell explains a higher level of leadership: "It's getting to know their people and figuring out how to get along with them. Leaders find out who their people are. Followers find out who their leaders are. People build solid, lasting relationships."[19] This is part of discipling. It includes but goes beyond teaching to knowing, as positive relationships are built with goals. Jesus' goals for his disciples were for them to love (worship) God with all their heart, soul, strength, and mind and love others enough to teach and disciple them to do the same.

Spending several years as a high school teacher, I understand that there is a general idea that teaching takes place in front of a classroom with students. Although worship leaders may be in situations where they teach in this kind of format, maybe in a Wednesday night class at church or smaller Sunday morning Bible study, the majority of teaching takes place in a different format. Worship leaders may teach in a standing circle as the worship team is tuning their instruments. They may teach in private counseling meetings. They may teach in a long conversation with an individual after the worship service or after a fellowship event. They may teach through mentoring and discipling one on one. They may teach with their example as many silent eyes watch from the distance. They may teach with their entire life by worshiping God through difficult life obstacles and tragedies. Some of the most powerful teachers are not those who teach with words but with time. They stay faithful through the tiring years and exemplify Christ's example in the Garden of Gethsemane where he requests the Father's will over his own in Luke chapter 22. They worry not about themselves but hold onto the attitude of Job when he says that even if God slays him, his hope is still in God in Job chapter 13. They live the reality of a hope that is only found in Jesus. He is our salvation. He is the only way.

Quality mentors are in scarcity. I can remember being in a Bible study as a young adult discussing with friends about how we wish we could find a mentor, someone to disciple us. If we could find someone who was willing, that person would often be a new believer, immature in the faith, and overzealous. The older, mature believers in the church were too busy to invest in some young kid right out of high school. I cannot recall how many times I have heard young adults express their desire for a good mentor and their frustration when they could not find one. Proverbs 13:20 states, "Whoever walks with the wise becomes wise, but the companion of fools will suffer harm."

It was in our mid-twenties when my best friend Chris and I were talking about our previous search to find an older, more spiritual mentor in the church. The church had people who were available to mentor recovering drug addicts, but there was not anyone for college students trying to navigate through a sometimes-confusing world. I remember distinctly when Chris looked at me with his serious face and said something that was a little scary to me: "Maybe it's our time to be the mentors." I knew we were not ready, but I understood that there was a need for us and others like us to step it up.

A few years ago at work in my art classroom, a student came up to me after a lecture on one of the elements of art. I noticed he did not bring up his sketchbook or pencil, so I was sure he was going to ask to use the restroom. He said, "Mr. Tripp, I was wondering ... well, I do not really have a dad, and I was wondering if I could ask you questions about life, like I would a dad?" He was asking me, in his own way, if I would be a mentor to him. I told him I would. The next day he brought in a suit catalog and asked me what type if suit should he rent for the prom. I looked through all of his circled options, and we discussed exactly what style he was looking for and what message he wanted to convey about himself at the prom. Did he want to be the cool guy who kept mysterious or the funny guy who stood out? In the last semester of the school year, he asked me questions about whether he should give a girl who he had a crush on a poem that he wrote for her. He asked me about life after high school and having a family. He asked me about prophecy and people at church. We talked about many things during those after-lecture class times when students were drawing and painting, and I got to tell him about God's love for him. He was not my best student. He did not even graduate high school on time. But he did go into the military, and the last time I heard from him, he seemed to be doing very well. He was one of the few who sought out a mentor. I worry about the masses who will never do such a thing but attempt to navigate through life alone. Most will not seek out people to mentor them and coach them through life. It is a vulnerable situation. It is not the norm. Such mentoring is a role that is seriously needed as the newer generations are raised with working parents, preoccupied parents, tired parents, single parents, and sometimes no parents.

Our ultimate goal of mentoring is to teach and disciple others to worship God. Therefore, mentees need to learn the foundation of Christian theology; they need to have an understanding of the attributes of God. In *The Attributes of God: Knowledge of the Holy*, A. W. Tozer states, "What comes into our minds when we think about God is the most important thing about us."[20] If people believe that God is an angry man upstairs just trying to punish them or believe God is not all-powerful, then they are going to worship him differently. As Christians, our confidence and hope does not come in the idea of believing in a god but believing in the one true God of the Bible.

At an art exhibition in Los Angeles, I ran into one of my old professors, and he asked what I had been up to. I informed him that I was taking some classes on worship studies. Knowing me as a visual artist, he said something like, "I didn't know you were into that stuff. Do you play in the band at your church or something?" He was an educated individual with the common layperson understanding that *worship* is music. True worship leaders have a responsibility to teach true worship. In *Worship through the Ages: How the Great Awakenings Shape Evangelical Worship*, Elmer Towns and Vernon Whaley explain, "True worship is not measured by the songs we sing; by the atmosphere, space, or environment we create in which to worship; by the number of Scriptures we read; or by the technology we deem important for facilitating worship. Worship is not determined by our preference for praise band, pipe organ, orchestra, or acoustic instruments."[21] They then explain how Jesus demonstrates the best definition of worship in what he called the greatest commandment in Mark 12:30. They state, "Biblical worship encompasses our heart's desire, our love for God, and our commitment to worship in spirit (our emotions) and in truth (our intellect). This kind of worship has been a part of every great spiritual awakening in history."[22] Worship involves a response from God, a change in the way we live. It is adapting our ways to his.

Right out of high school, I played in a Christian ska band that was active in California. It was during the popularity of ska music with bands like O.C. Supertones, Five Iron Frenzy, and The Insyderz. We were called Skalastix, which was fitting for the time since we were all college age teens. We played at churches and secular venues. The band was full of a variety of unique believers who were eager to share the gospel with others. Finding out we were Christians, some would respond in spite. I remember one girl say, "I worship Satan." When someone makes such a statement, what does it really mean? Was she saying that she spends about half an hour singing worship songs to Satan one or two times a week? It most likely means she attempts to follow the ways of Satan. The contrast I have witnessed is that some Christians think they can worship God but not follow his ways. Worshiping God shapes us to be devoted followers of Jesus. True worship is about obeying God—following him. At times Christians worship using music, but music is often a small part of the lifestyle worship that God requires.

I saw a sign on a church before that read: "No perfect people permitted." The point being that there are imperfect people at church; there are sinners at church. Although this is true, it is still difficult to see people sing loudly with raised hands during musical worship and then seeing the same person an hour later display a lack of lifestyle worship during lunch. Such sights are difficult for believers and non-believers alike because even the non-believer understands that worship is more than music and singing. Worship leaders, specifically musical worship leaders, have the responsibility to teach and disciple others to understand true worship. Although music is a very powerful tool to help us glorify God as we focus on him, there is so much more. Christians thinking that worship only takes place musically a few times a week is a dangerous false idea that misguides the church away from being lifestyle worshipers.

THE WORSHIP LEADER'S OUTREACH ROLE

A lthough staying active and busy in the church may seem to be the rightful place for worship leaders to dwell, worship leaders are also called to be present in leading outreach. Throughout modern church history, preachers traveled with musicians as effective teams to share the gospel of Christ. There is a special and unique characteristic about music that helps guide people to the truth when it is done right. Colossians 3:16-17 states, "Let the word of Christ dwell in you richly, teaching and admonishing one another in all wisdom, singing psalms and hymns and spiritual songs, with thankfulness in your hearts to God. And whatever you do, in word or deed, do everything in the name of the Lord Jesus, giving thanks to God the Father through him." With Scripture as a foundation, we create music for glorifying God, which also helps guide us to live a lifestyle of worship in everything we do. Music as a holy artform can bring separated people together. It can instantly change moods and connect strangers. I have witnessed this at the Los Angeles Dodger's stadium. With people sitting in nose-bleed sections with tickets they won through a radio show and others sitting in prime seating that cost thousands, when Journey's "Don't Stop

Believin'" came on, everyone sang along in united energy. Worship leaders can use the same artform of music to bring together different people from different communities for the purpose of glorifying God. In God's Big Picture: Tracing the Storyline of the Bible, Vaughan Roberts shares, "When I go to a classical music concert, I am always amazed that an orchestra, which consists of so many individuals with very different instruments, can combine to produce such a beautiful sound."[23] Even the idea of composing music can be an analogy of the church—different people coming together to make something beautiful.

Growing up as a teenager in Bakersfield, California, the home of Buck Owens and Korn, many of my friends played in a band. It was what we did on Friday and Saturday nights. In the late 90s, the alternative rock band was just plain cool. There was still music on MTV where teens watched music videos of Collective Soul, Stone Temple Pilots, and The Smashing Pumpkins in between episodes of *Beavis and Butt-Head* and *Daria*. As a young teen, I can remember standing with my grandfather's red electric guitar around me staring into the reflection of my grandparents' refrigerator and being intrigued by the imaginative possibilities such an instrument could bring. Mid-high school when I joined my first rock band, I was given access to that local stage light, and it would be my passion for many years to come. Pastors and worship leaders at local churches grabbed hold of the youth's musical passion and began to hold concerts at churches. In my town there were often multiple concert options to attend every weekend. With my love for music, I spent much of those teen years fellowshipping with other believers who shared the same passion for music, and I saw many who gave their lives to Christ through such events because leaders in churches valued outreach.

I am not sure the hype of the concert scene will ever fully return, but there are other musical ways for worship leaders to lead outreach. Worship nights can allow people in the community to come to church in a less formal setting. Worship nights can differ from the Sunday worship service in atmosphere and style. Lights can be dim. Candles can be present. Music can be more of a contemporary and experimental style. Extra time can be allowed for group prayer. The entire setting can just be more relaxed and open. People can fellowship afterwards and even go out for a late dinner to build relationships. Sometimes people just need a place to go and spend time in prayer in the right environment. People can surely worship God anywhere. College students will go to the library or Starbucks with earphones to get away from distractions to be in the right environment for better focus. Worship nights can be a short spiritual retreat from the busy and distracting life of stacking tasks and responsibilities. This is in no way a replacement for the Sunday morning worship service but a short time of refocus. Such worship nights can be more artistic for the purpose of pointing to God. In *Worship Old and New: A Biblical, Historical, and Practical Introduction*, Robert Webber states,

> Thus, the artist in the service of God (the creator) displays redemption through artistic creativity and sets creation free to worship God. Therefore, environmental art, the visual arts, and the movement arts are not primarily presentational or witness arts in worship, but acts of worship that serve the goal of pointing all of creation toward the praise of God.[24]

With allowed and encouraged creativity, worship nights can be a safe place to try out new artistic environments to help visually and even emotionally point all the focus to God.

The worship leader can help lead outreach with charitable events as well. Holidays offer convenient opportunities for the church to hold food drives and clothing distribution. These are good events to team up with other local churches since deeper theological differences can be left out of donating food and clothing. The worship leader can even find ways to musically lead during such events. Many drives that I have been a part of have had a musical element to them. A simple acoustic set up in the background can add to the overall mood and environment of such charitable events. This is also more warming for those who are receiving the charity. With some proper planning of musical elements, the event can be turned into a happy time of receiving instead of a shameful time of needing. Giving should be done in joy and receiving should be encouraging and uplifting to those who are in need.

Worship leaders can also lead in outreach with more solemn situations in the local community. During sad times of tragedy, worship leaders can volunteer to provide music of comfort and hope. Although people are not as eager to lead in such events like funerals, prayer vigils, and memorials, such events can be important areas of outreach. My family began attending church when I was in the 6th grade after my aunt died. The pastor who conducted my aunt's funeral was so caring and kind, my parents and grandparents wanted to attend her church. It was a great starting point for a family who had not regularly attended church and who would later become very much involved.

Overall, outreach should not be placed into its own category outside of worship. Webber explains, "Worship is, therefore, not only an inner heartfelt response of thanksgiving; it also indicates a life totally committed to serving God."[25] Worship is a response of God's love that moves us to serve him with every aspect of our life. Worship leaders do not just serve during musical worship practices and during the worship service. They are like a tree that branches out into many different directions, bearing fruit with nutrients that restore and heal. The worship leader does not say, "My job is to just handle the music," or "Outreach is for the missionaries." Just as a tree reaches out its branches, worship leaders reach out to help guide the lost to Christ. They leave the ninety-nine to go after the one who is lost, for this glorifies God. This is worship.

THE WORSHIP LEADER'S ROLE OF AN ADVOCATE OF THE ARTS

I magine a society where the hub of the creative arts was the church and people came to church to learn, develop, and practice such artforms. Music, theatre, and visual art are all elements of God's creation. They were created and exist with a practical purpose to bring glory to God. Just like anything God has created for good, the enemy aims to turn it around for evil—for self. People have found ways to use the creative arts for self-glorification instead of worshiping God. Romans 1:21-23 states: "For although they knew God, they did not honor him as God or give thanks to him, but they became futile in their thinking, and their foolish hearts were darkened. Claiming to be wise, they became fools, and exchanged the glory of the immortal God for images resembling mortal man and birds and animals and creeping things." This section of Romans describes the modern culture of the arts, as people give up truth for worshiping the creation rather than the creator. The loss of such creative arts in church is partially at the fault of Christians. In Worship, Old and New:

A Biblical, Historical, and Practical Introduction, Robert Webber states, "The Reformers, particularly Calvin and Zwingli, viewed the arts as worldly and as having no place in the church and in its worship."[26]

When I think about the loss of the creative arts in church, I think of a story about a father, his son, and a car. There was once a father who knew his son was getting closer to the driving age, so he started fixing up a classic car for him to drive. He fixed up the car to make it safe and productive but also to be enjoyable. When his son turned sixteen, his father handed over the keys. Later out of a fear of driving, the boy gave the car away to others who would drive it dangerously, putting everyone on the road at risk. Webber explains, "The twentieth-century Protestant church woke up to the unfortunate realization that by its neglect of the visual arts, drama, and dance the world now owned what rightfully belonged to the church."[27] It is time for the church to take back the creative arts and use them for their created purpose of worship. Being leaders with a creative calling, worship leaders have the role of leading such a task. This will be a true challenge because not only will the world fight against this idea, but people in the church will as well. Even good change is change, and unfortunately, there are many who are stubbornly defiant to try anything out of their traditional comfort zone.

Many people today do not know that the first forms on modern musical notation were developed by monks in churches to create standardize liturgy. Before that music was used powerfully with David as he commanded it of the Levites in 1 Chronicles 15:16: "David also commanded the chiefs of the Levites to appoint their brothers as the singers who should play loudly on musical instruments, on harps and lyres and cymbals, to raise sounds of joy." Growing up as a teenager in the 1990s, a lot of music was associated with evil with the popularization of heavy metal bands and rap music. Musical lyrics questioned God's attributes of goodness and faithfulness and added lyrics that were often oversexualized and profane. When a fellow musician friend of mine and I were looking for music studios to rent in college, we checked out one cheap studio that was underground below a music store downtown. The store's owner said he would let us rent it for a discounted price because the heavy metal band that used to rent it would cut themselves and sprinkle their blood on the walls in some form of satanic ritual. My friend, who was a solid believer, and I set up our guitar amps and just played together in that decrepit studio. It felt like our clean guitar tones formed together in unity to clear the darkness. We did not talk much but just played for about forty-five minutes. We both left agreeing that the studio space was not for us.

Growing up I always heard from people that sex, drugs, and rock'n roll were the tools of the devil. Being a passionate musician, it hurt my heart knowing that something as good as music had been tainted to be a tool of destruction, but something changed in the 1990s as I rode with my father in our family's minivan. "Jesus Freak" by DC Talk played over the radio, and for the first time, I heard Christian music that sounded better than popular secular music. As more Christians in rock bands came out to take over the stage, Christians began to take a form of music back and have continued to do so today.

Other creative arts have not been so fortunate. Theatre and acting are often associated with Hollywood, which is known for being a hub of sinful activity. In a lot of cities and towns, the theatre community is known for being far removed from biblical values. I have witnessed some churches attempt and sometimes excel in producing strong theatrical productions around Christmas and Easter, but for the most part, if people want to be involved with acting, they must go elsewhere. Churches have the space for such theatrical productions with a stage, sound equipment, lighting, seating, etc. Often churches are more equipped for productions than small community theaters. With the amount of talent and skill from spirit-led Christians in the local church, worship leaders and pastors can utilize the church building to produce theatrical performances that challenge the local community to worship God in spirit and in truth. Just like how a good novel uses storytelling to share a theme, the same can happen with a performance as biblical themes and instruction can lead people to Christ. In *Can't Wait for Sunday: Leading Your Congregation in Authentic Worship*, Michael Walters explains, "Theologians have held for centuries that the artistic impulse, the desire to create works of beauty and imagination, is a part of our God-given impulse to worship. Thus, to separate art and worship is to violate the intent of the Creator himself."[28] Such theatrical productions would be works of the imagination created for the purpose of bringing people together to glorify God through the art of theatre.

Some may be eager to resist the idea of having dramatized events take place in the church, but in *Worship Old and New: A Biblical, Historical, and Practical Introduction*, Robert Webber explains that dramatized acting is already a positive part of Christian worship: "Historical orientation also underlines New Testament worship. Christian worship derives from the death and resurrection of Christ. In preaching we retell the story: in the Eucharist we dramatize the event. Even worship on Sunday has significance in terms of enactment, for that is the day of the Resurrection."[29] Obviously, a theatrical performance would look different than the regular worship service, but acting is still involved with the purpose of biblically bringing glory to God through teaching, outreach, and encouragement.

Visual art is often neglected in the Protestant church, leaving artists to venture out into the art world for community. In Michael Walters' *Can't Wait for Sunday: Leading Your Congregation in Authentic Worship, Walters* states, "The fact that art has had difficulty finding acceptance, particularly within conservative Protestantism, says something about both the church's failure to heed its own doctrine of Creation and the propensity of human beings to turn for evil purposes the good gifts of the Creator."[30] From my experiences as an exhibiting visual artist in the Los Angeles area, some of the art community is full of very kind and supportive people, but other parts are very dark. I attended an art exhibition once where there were life-size, human-shaped sculptures. One of the curators explained to me that the sculptural pieces were demi-gods and demons. Visual art being used to exalt demons is far from how it used to visually tell stories from Scripture.

Historically, visual art was used in corporate worship. In *A Brief History of Christian Worship*, James White explains church art history:

> Most of our earliest surviving liturgical art was associated with burial of the dead. Not surprisingly, it featured resurrection themes, often in Old Testament terms: Jonah and the whale, Daniel and the boys in the fiery furnace, the raising of Lazarus. Occasionally Christ is portrayed as the Good Shepherd or the Church as a praying woman. The cross does not appear until the fourth century and then often with a lamb on it. Not until the end of the seventh century do we discover the familiar crucifix. After the Marian debates at the Council of Ephesus in 431, figures of Mary became prominent. The churches were learning a new visual vocabulary, one image at a time. By the end of the patristic period many images had become familiar for visual expression in worship.[31]

Such visual art was not only for expression but for the visual presentation of Scripture with the telling of the stories of the disciples, the life of Christ, and the second coming, along with much more. For a time when many were illiterate, visual images helped share truth.

With the common and active presence of social media, video games, and movies, our society today is very much a visual one. In *Worship: Old and New*, Robert Webber states, "Thus, the artist in the service of God (the creator) displays redemption through artistic creativity and sets creation free to worship God. Therefore, environmental art, the visual arts, and the movement arts are not primarily presentational or witness arts in worship, but acts of worship that serve the goal of pointing all of creation toward the praise of God."[32] Unfortunately, visual art along with other creative arts are often not allowed or encouraged in the modern church, and people feel they need to leave church to seek their calling to create.

In *A Brief History of Christian Worship*, James White states,

"We do not yet have enough varieties of Christian worship. What can be done to help liturgically disenfranchised groups to express their worship of the Christian God in forms that are natural to them? How do such groups learn to be themselves in their worship of Jesus Christ?"[33] Imagine the society where when people wanted to be creative, they went to church. If we are made in the image of God—the greatest creator—there should be more ways to be creative in church. People should not feel they have to join a different community to be a musician, actor, or artist. Senior pastors are not always known for being the most artistic leaders in the church, but worship leaders are naturally more involved and have the role of being an advocate of the arts. Being an advocate of the arts is being an advocate of those who God has called to be creatives. It is advocating for them to be creative in ways that bring glory to God. It helps them be less about themselves and more about God through creative means. It helps teach others through artistic creations with the focus always being on Jesus.

THE WORSHIP LEADER'S ROLE OF SERVANTHOOD

J esus is clear in Mark 9:35: "Anyone who wants to be first must be the very last, and the servant of all." This is sometimes the secret struggle for many leaders because they often have an inner desire to be first. They want to be seen. They want to be heard. They desire the stage. In Overcoming the Dark Side of Leadership: The Paradox of Personal Dysfunction, Gary McIntosh and Samuel Rima state, "Narcissistic leaders are driven to succeed by a need for admiration and acclaim. They may have an overinflated sense of importance as well as great ambitions and grandiose fantasies."[34] Such leaders feel an overwhelming since of importance of their goals and feel that only they can make them happen, not trusting in God for accomplishment but in their own abilities instead. By placing such high importance upon themselves, they often feel underappreciated, which creates deep feelings of inferiority that are overcompensated by other behaviors, some good and some bad. To avoid narcissistic thoughts, worship leaders should remind themselves of the attributes of God, specifically God's sovereignty. God does not need us; he chooses to use us to allow us to be a part of the blessing of his holy work. We are the servant. To be an authentic minister of reconciliation and one who leads the world to worship in spirit and truth, we must daily remind ourselves of our true identity in Christ—a child of God, a holy servant to advance his kingdom.

One of the most destructive traits of a worship leader is pride. Proverbs 16:5 states, "Everyone who is arrogant in heart is an abomination to the Lord; be assured, he will not go unpunished." In Isaiah 14:13-14, we see the scary *I will* statements made by the enemy: "I will ascend to heaven; above the stars of God I will set my throne on high; I will sit on the mount of assembly in the far reaches of the north; I will ascend above the heights of the clouds; I will make myself like the Most High." Too often I have heard the similar *I will* statements of pride from the mouths of Christian preceding their fall. Now, there is no need to be legalistic and never use the words *I will* or always state *God willing* at the end of your statements. We should be able to state, "I will order the chicken sandwich" without being attacked by a legalistic person. The matter of importance is in the heart. We must ask the challenging question, "Does all of my heart's desire bow down to the will of God?" This is the essence of a true servant and worshiper of God.

Worship leaders should be eager to serve when there is a need and when they are available. This does not mean that worship leaders should be bossed around every which way by anyone and everyone. They should have their main responsibilities and roles that they are committed to, but beyond those responsibilities, worship leaders should be willing to step in and work when needed. In *The Unbelievable Gospel: Say Something Worth Believing*, Jonathan Dodson states, "Christian work should be excellent and innovative. We should always seek to improve, to bless, and to serve others through our work."[35] Our horizontal lifestyle of servanthood with God's creation is one of the clearest indicators of our vertical worship to God. I remember being around thirteen years old and helping my parents put away folding chairs after a church event. My mother asked a man standing around if he would like to help. He responded that he would have to pray about whether God wants him to help. This situation will always stand out in my memory of someone who did not have a heart of a servant. God wants us to serve. He wants us to help those who need it. This is not a complex issue. Serving is a natural response to us taking in the Word of God and being filled with the Holy Spirit.

On the night Jesus was betrayed, Jesus partook in the Passover meal with his disciples. No servant was present to wash the men's feet. Not long after some of the disciples were arguing about who would be the greatest in the kingdom of God, they all ignored the belittling task, except Jesus. He did not have to pray about it first. He did not have to be on the official feet-washing ministry. He did not say, "Now you owe me," or "This is really bad timing." Jesus simply served.

Looking over the city of a very high mountain, Jesus had the devil leave him by stating, "You shall worship the Lord your God and him only shall you serve" (Matthew 4:8-10). Some people are servants, but they are servants to themselves, servants to sin. They may be dedicated, devoted, faithful, and reliable, but to the wrong thing. In *Called to Worship: The Biblical Foundations of Our Response to God's Call*, Vernon Whaley explains about God: "He created humanity to *worship*, and he gave us the principles to do so through the act of Creation."[36] Living as beings who are created to worship, we will all worship and serve something. It may be education or a career. It may be a relationship or reputation. It may be a band or football team. It may be ourselves. We as humans need to fulfil the natural void we have to worship and serve. If our main purpose in life is to serve anything besides the eternal God of the Bible, our lives will be spent in vain and in misery. Only God can fill our void.

It is with our service that we worship God and lead others to worship him. It is our response from being changed by his Holy Word and through the guidance of the Holy Spirit that we worship God in spirit and in truth. With our identity being in Christ as a child of God, we grow in our calling as worship leaders. We have failed and will fail in the future, but we rest in the salvation of Jesus Christ knowing that in him there is no condemnation

(Romans 8:1). We are free, and as ministers of reconciliation, we help others find that same freedom and regained an innocence that is only found in Christ. It is the good news, the gospel. And we have been given leadership and pastoral roles to help others know and understand the good news and to accept it to fulfil their own calling as worshipers of the one true God, living out worship that is so much more than a Sunday morning service, living out worship that is their entire lifestyle as a child of God.

References

Clinton, Timothy E., and Ronald E. Hawkins. *The Quick-Reference Guide to Biblical Counseling*. Grand Rapids, MI: Baker, 2009.

Cottrell, Jack. *Baptism: A Biblical Study*. Joplin, MO: College Press Publishing Company, 2015.

Davis, John Jefferson. *Worship and the Reality of God: An Evangelical Theology of Real Presence*. Downers Grove, IL: IVP Academic, 2010.

Dodson, Jonathan K. *The Unbelievable Gospel: Say Something Worth Believing*. Grand Rapids, MI: Vondervan, 2014.

Due, Noel. *Created for Worship: From Genesis to Revelation to You*. Fearn, Ross-Shire, Scotland: Christian Focus, 2005.

MacArthur, John. *Worship: The Ultimate Priority*. Chicago, IL: Moody Publishers, 2012.

Mathena, Gary. *One Thing Needful an Invitation to the Study of Worship*. Bloomington, IN: West Bow Press, 2016.

Maxwell, John C. *How Successful People Lead: Taking Your Influence to the Next Level*. New York, NY: Center Street, 2013.

Maxwell, John C. *The 5 Levels of Leadership: Proven Steps to Maximize Your Potential*. New York, NY: Center Street, 2011.

McIntosh, Gary L., and Samuel D. Rima. *Overcoming the Dark Side of Leadership: The Paradox of Personal Dysfunction*. Grand Rapids, MI: Baker Books, 2000.

Miller, Stephen. *Worship Leaders: We Are Not Rock Stars*. Chicago, IL: Moody Publishers, 2013.

Peterson, David. *Engaging with God: A Biblical Theology of Worship*. Downers Grove, IL: InterVarsity Press, 2004.

Sanders, Oswald J. *Spiritual Leadership: Principles of Excellence for Every Believer*. Chicago, IL: Moody Publishers, 2017.

Towns, Elmer L. and Vernon M. Whaley. *Worship Through the Ages: How the Great Awakenings Shape Evangelical Worship.* Nashville, TN: B & H Academic, 2012.

Tozer, A. W. *The Attributes of God: The Knowledge of the Holy.* New York, NY: Walker, 1996.

Roberts, Vaughn. *God's Big Picture: Tracing the Storyline of the Bible.* Downers Grove, IL: Intervarsity Press, 2002.

Walters, J. Michael. *Can't Wait for Sunday: Leading Your Congregation in Authentic Worship.* Indianapolis, IN: Wesleyan Publishing House, 2006.

Webber, Robert. *Worship, Old and New.* Seoul, Korea: Publishing House, The Presbyterian Church of Korea, 1988.

Willard, Dallas. *The Allure of Gentleness: Defending the Faith in the Manner of Jesus.* Sydney, NSW 2000: HarperCollins, 2015.

Williams, Dave. *How to Help Your Pastor Succeed: Moving from the Multitude to the Inner Circle.* Monroe, MI: Decapolis Publishing, 2008.

Whaley, Vernon. *Called to Worship: The Biblical Foundations of Our Response to God's Call.* Nashville, TN: Thomas Nelson, 2013.

White, James Emery. *The Church in an Age of Crisis: 25 New Realities Facing Christianity.* Grand Rapids, MI: Baker Books, 2012.

White, James F. *A Brief History of Christian Worship.* Nashville, TN: Abingdon Press, 1993.

---

[1] Jack Cottrell, *Baptism: A Biblical Study* (Joplin, MO: College Press Publishing Company, 2015), 163, Kindle.

[2] John MacArthur, *Worship: The Ultimate Priority* (Chicago, IL: Moody Publishers, 2012), 14.

[3] Ibid., 10.

[4] James Emery White. *The Church in an Age of Crisis: 25 New Realities Facing Christianity.* (Grand Rapids, MI: Baker Books, 2012), 25, Kindle.

[5] J. Oswald Sanders, *Spiritual Leadership: Principles of Excellence for Every Believer.* (Chicago, IL: Moody Publishers, 2007), 49, Kindle.

[6] Stephen Miller. *Worship Leaders, We are Not Rock Stars.* (Chicago, IL: Moody Publishers, 2013), 120, Kindle.

[7] J. Oswald Sanders, *Spiritual Leadership: Principles of Excellence for Every Believer.* (Chicago, IL: Moody Publishers, 2007), 49, Kindle.

[8] Michael Walters, *Can't Wait for Sunday: Leading Your Congregation in Authentic Worship.* (Indianapolis, IN: Wesleyan Publishing House, 2006), 616, Kindle.

[9] Dave Williams, *How to Help Your Pastor Succeed: Moving from the Multitude to the Inner Circle* (Monroe, MI: Decapolis Publishing, 2008), 1570, Kindle.

[10] Ibid.

[11] John Maxwell, *How Successful People Lead: Taking Your Influence to the Next Level* (New York, NY: Center Street, 2013), 47, Kindle.

[12] Stephen Miller. *Worship Leaders, We are Not Rock Stars.* (Chicago, IL: Moody Publishers, 2013), 70, Kindle.

[13] Vernon Whaley, *Called to Worship: The Biblical Foundations of Our Response to Gods Call.* (Nashville, TN: Thomas Nelson, 2009), 3, Kindle.

[14] Gary L. McIntosh and Samuel D. Rima, *Overcoming the Dark Side of Leadership: The Paradox of Personal Dysfunction* (Grand Rapids, MI: Baker Books, 2000), 2562, Kindle.

[15] Ibid., 2569.

[16] Timothy E. Clinton and Ronald E. Hawkins, *The Quick-Reference Guide to Biblical Counseling* (Grand Rapids, MI: Baker, 2009), 101, Kindle.

[17] Ibid., 108.

[18] John MacArthur, *Worship: The Ultimate Priority* (Chicago, IL: Moody Publishers, 2012), 22.

[19] John C. Maxwell, *The 5 Levels of Leadership: Proven Steps to Maximize Your Potential* (New York, NY: Center Street, 2011), 8, Kindle.

[20] A. W. Tozer, *The Attributes of God: The Knowledge of the Holy* (New York, NY: Walker, 1996), 72, Kindle.

[21] Elmer Towns and Vernon Whaley, *Worship Through the Ages: How the Great Awakenings Shape Evangelical Worship* (Nashville, TN: B & H Academic, 2012), 158, Kindle.

[22] Ibid., 181.

[23] Vaughan Roberts, *God's Big Picture: Tracing the Storyline of the Bible* (Downers Grove, IL: InterVarsity Press, 2002), 1303, Kindle.

[24] Robert Webber, *Worship, Old and New* (Seoul, Korea: Publishing House, The Presbyterian Church of Korea, 1988), 3878, Kindle.

[25] Robert Webber, *Worship, Old and New* (Seoul, Korea: Publishing House, The Presbyterian Church of Korea, 1988), 439, Kindle.

[26] Robert Webber, *Worship, Old and New: A Biblical, Historical, and Practical Introduction* (Seoul, Korea: Publishing House, The Presbyterian Church of Korea, 1988), 3958.

[27] Ibid., 3969.

[28] J. Michael, Walters, *Can't Wait for Sunday: Leading Your Congregation in Authentic Worship* (Indianapolis, IN: Wesleyan Publishing House, 2006). 2249, Kindle.
[29]
       Robert Webber, *Worship, Old and New: A Biblical, Historical, and Practical Introduction* (Seoul, Korea: Publishing House, The Presbyterian Church of Korea, 1988), 1243.

[30] J. Michael Walters, *Can't Wait for Sunday: Leading Your Congregation in Authentic Worship* (Indianapolis, IN: Wesleyan Publishing House, 2006). 2280, Kindle.

[31] James White, *A Brief History of Christian Worship* (Nashville, TN: Abingdon Press, 1993), 73-74, Kindle.

[32] Robert Webber, *Worship, Old and New* (Seoul, Korea: Publishing House, The Presbyterian Church of Korea, 1988), 3875.

[33] James White, *A Brief History of Christian Worship* (Nashville, TN: Abingdon Press, 1993), 179, Kindle.

[34] Gary L. McIntosh and Samuel D. Rima, *Overcoming the Dark Side of Leadership: The Paradox of Personal Dysfunction* (Grand Rapids, MI: Baker Books, 2000), 1437, Kindle.

[35] Jonathan K. Dodson, *The Unbelievable Gospel: Say Something Worth Believing,* (Grand Rapids, MI: Vondervan, 2014), 42, Kindle.

[36] Vernon Whaley, *Called to Worship: The Biblical Foundations of Our Response to God's Call* (Nashville, TN: Thomas Nelson, 2013), 8, Kindle.

ABOUT THE AUTHOR

Terry Tripp

Terry Tripp is a teacher, writer, artist, and musician in Southern California. He played on his first worship team at the age of twelve and has always been passionately curious about the topic of worship. Tripp graduated from California State University, Bakersfield with a BA in English and a BA in Psychology and earned an MA in Education from Point Loma Nazarene University and an MFA in Visual Art from Azusa Pacific University.

BOOKS BY THIS AUTHOR

I Believe In Silence

During the twilight evening, Theodore London walks his college campus with suicidal thoughts brought on by his present life, remembering the simple memories of his youth. He realizes that he misses the innocence of days gone by. Theodore is thinking about how he will kill himself, and he has thirteen pills in his pocket to accomplish the deadly task when he sees a young girl who appears as a ghostly figure in the distance.

My Cold Autumn Sky

Crossing the bridge between poetry and the human experience, Terry Tripp presents an imaginative collection of poetry that resonates with the youthful heart by sharing bits and pieces of life's inevitable pain and wondrous joys. This collection is poetry for the courageous thinker—one who approaches the mysteries of life without fear and who finds the beauty that is often hidden in a sometimes-confusing world. Tripp writes about heartfelt topics, such as love, faith, truth, mortality, and reconciliation in his poems, challenging his readers to find their own childlike innocence.

Christmas Land: And Other Seasonal Stories

After Cindy loses her grandmother, the young graphic designer in her twenties faces the yuletide season alone in the small mountain town of Timberton Heights. This Christmas will be unlike any other as she uncovers the magical land of Christmas. Classic legends meet modern day reality in this new seasonal novel of Christmas adventure that will help anyone get into the Christmas spirit. Terry Tripp's collection of short stories touches upon the wistfulness of the Christmas season as they span the spectrum of human thought and emotion, leaving readers in a pensive state of awe. Tripp pushes his readers to meditate upon life, death, love, and family in these touching holiday tales.

Printed in Great Britain
by Amazon